50 THINGS ANIMALS CAN TEACH US

Ron Ovadia

Animal and Story Consultant: Jackie Ovadia

Life HIGHPOINT

This edition published by Highpoint Life, an imprint of Highpoint Executive Publishing. For information, write to info@highpointpubs.com.

First Edition
ISBN: 979-8-9862590-6-2

Ovadia, Ron
50 Things Animals Can Teach Us

Cover and interior design by Sarah Clarehart

"Animals can teach us many things, from life lessons to everyday wisdom. This book captures 50 such lessons from some of the most fascinating creatures in the world, illustrated through stunning photographs." – Provided by Publisher

ISBN: 979-8-9862590-6-2 (Hardcover)
1. Children 2. Animals

Library of Congress Control Number: 2022917359

Manufactured in the United States of America

DEDICATION

Dedicated to everyone who works with animals, cares for animals, helps protect animals in the wild, has an animal as a family member—and most of all, to the children who love animals.

CONTENTS

INTRODUCTION

Animals can teach us many things, from life lessons to everyday wisdom. I have tried to capture 50 examples, drawing upon 54 animals. In nearly all cases, they are rooted in zoological facts. But in some instances, I have taken some creative license to serve a lesson. Hopefully, animal science purists won't take issue with my occasional diversion and will appreciate my overriding intention to find relevant lessons for children, even if the animal link seems… a little fishy.

HOW TO READ THIS BOOK
This book is not intended to be read cover to cover. You'll want to enjoy and appreciate each animal and what they can teach us. Feel free to start with your favorite animals. Parents and children are also encouraged to share each lesson to make the learning experience even richer.

There's so much you can learn
If you know where to turn
Besides your mom and dad
and all your teachers
Right there in the zoo
In the wild and your home, too
Lessons you can learn from many creatures

So come and take a look
At the animals in this book
The more you know
the more you will respect them
They can be your faithful friends
But their survival can depend
On all of us helping to protect them

ANT

YOU GET MORE DONE WITH TEAMWORK

Ants work very hard, more than anyone
And working with each other, they get so much done

Ants are the hardest-working creatures. They can even carry 10 to 50 times their body weight. (Don't try that!) Ants also work together to complete tasks. If you try to be as productive as an ant and work in teams, you'll get much more done and learn that almost anything is possible.

APE

HUMANS AREN'T THE ONLY INTELLIGENT ANIMALS

If you think humans are the only ones who're smart
Take a look at apes, and that is just a start

Apes, including chimps, are very intelligent. They communicate, solve problems, and can learn language. They are also social and live in close families. A cousin of humans, apes show us that we are not the only highly intelligent animal. It also feels good getting credit for being smart.

BEAR

PROTECT THE ENVIRONMENT

Bears are mighty creatures,
vital to the forest

Helping it to thrive as nature's own florist

Bears fertilize forests with salmon skeletons, fruits, seeds, and their own poop—at least when they're not hibernating to conserve energy in the winter, when food is scarce. Bears help preserve the environment. Think about what you might do to preserve our precious planet.

BEAVER

TRYING HARD PAYS OFF

Beavers build their dams with branches in streams
Reminding you to work hard to reach your goals and dreams

Beavers build dams to create a pond where they can build a protected home. They never stop rebuilding their dams, even when they are damaged by rain or floods. The way they always try, even when things are hard, makes beavers special. That's a good lesson for getting stuff done.

BEE

PROTECT THOSE WHO SUPPORT LIFE ITSELF

Bees are busy pollinating flowers; it's so neat!
They help produce a lot of fruits and vegetables we eat

Bees deposit pollen in plants, which allows the plants to create seeds that grow into new plants. This helps produce much of the world's food! Bees are needed for nature's delicate balance. We must "bee" sure to keep them safe by not using chemicals in our gardens.

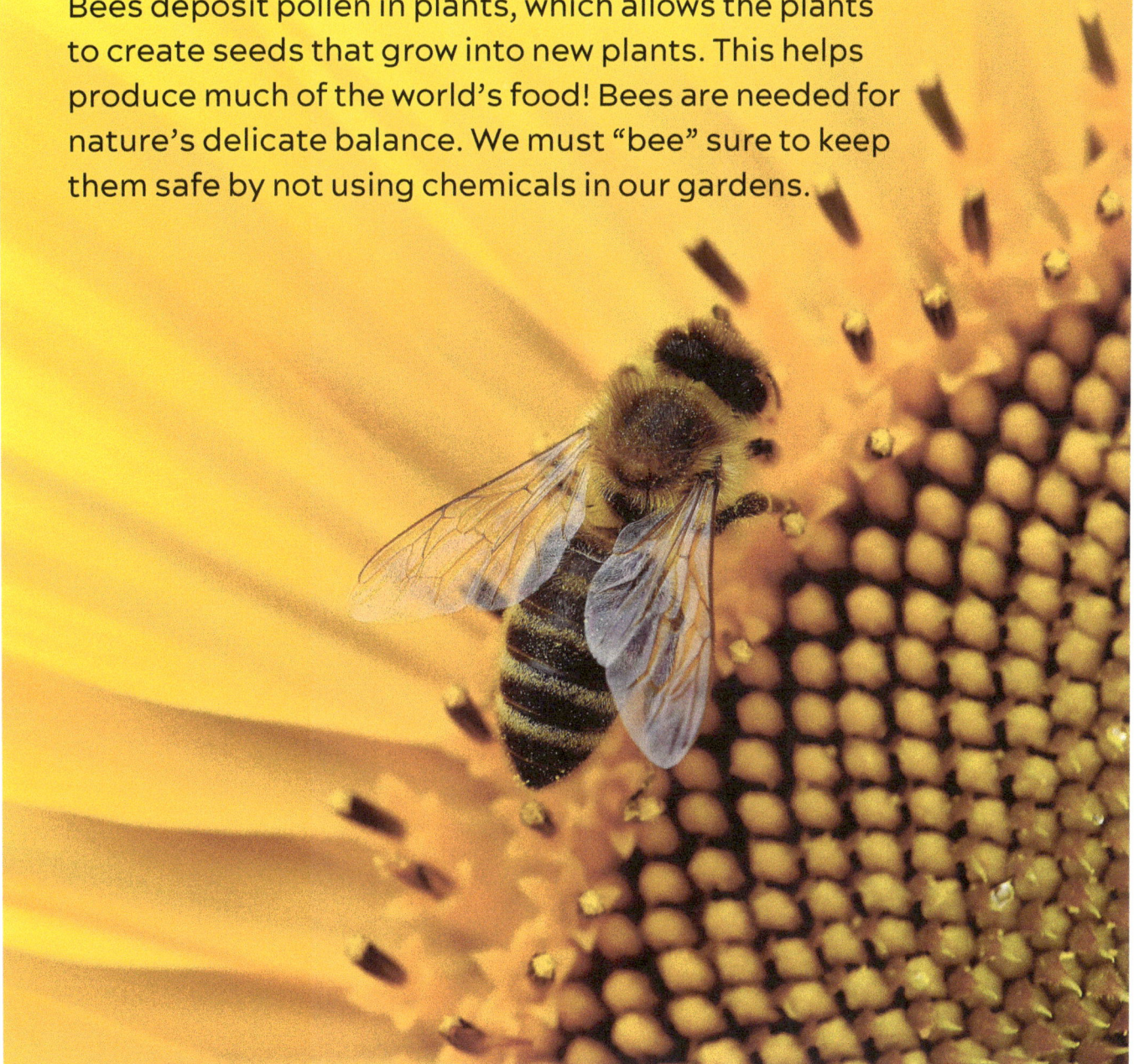

BUTTERFLY

CHANGE IS ESSENTIAL TO LIFE

The way that butterflies grow is such a wondrous thing.
From egg to caterpillar to the time they spread their wings!

Butterflies develop through a process of change called metamorphosis. Adult female butterflies lay eggs. A caterpillar hatches from the egg. It eats, grows, and forms a chrysalis, which splits. Out comes a beautiful butterfly and a lesson: Change is essential to life; that's how you grow!

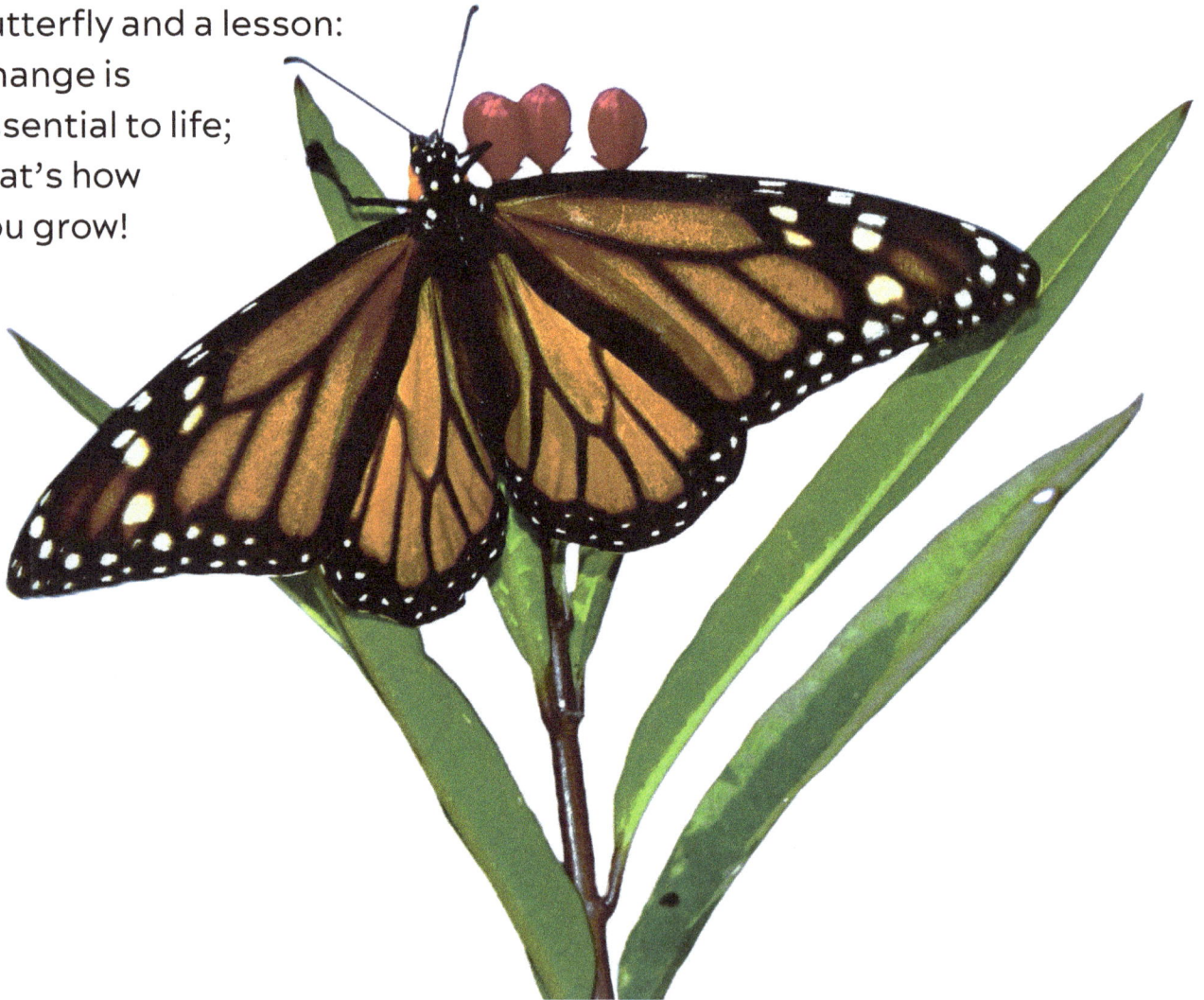

CAMEL

DRINK A LOT OF WATER, ESPECIALLY WHEN IT'S HOT

In the desert heat, there's no place that is hotter
That's why camels drink and store soooooooo much water

Did you know your body is made up of two-thirds water?
That's why it's so important to drink plenty of water. Camels
remind us of this. To survive in the desert, they drink up to 50
gallons of water at once and store it. You need to drink plenty
of water, too, especially in hot weather.

CAT

IT'S IMPORTANT TO KNOW HOW
TO MAKE PEOPLE FEEL GOOD

Cats are friendly pets with soft and soothing fur
They can win your heart with their vibrating purr

No animal sound is as calming and comforting as a cat's purr. Cats often purr when they feel good—and only with humans. They've learned that purrrrrring is comforting to people and a way to connect with them. How can you communicate with others to make them feel good?

CATERPILLAR

SOMETIMES YOU DON'T GET THE CREDIT YOU DESERVE

Want to know "the wind beneath a butterfly's wings?"
The caterpillar, they do almost everything

Butterflies get all the glory. But what about caterpillars? These eating machines do almost all the work, constantly munching on leaves to get the energy to complete the metamorphosis. The lesson? Do your work, quietly, and eventually, people will see the beauty of what you've done.

COW

IF YOU'RE HAPPY, YOU'LL BE MORE PRODUCTIVE

Cows produce the milk children like to drink a lot
And when the cows are happy, the taste hits the spot!

Thank cows for the fresh milk you get. But treat them well, and you get an even bigger treat! Happier cows that are more content around farmers produce better milk than stressed cows—and far more of it. When you are happy, you are more productive.

DEER

APPRECIATE SILENCE AND STILLNESS

Deer remind us just how quiet and peaceful life can be
And that we must appreciate animals that are free

Deer live in safe, wooded areas where they can avoid predators. These beautiful animals are quiet, calm, and graceful. They remind us how peaceful life can be. Appreciate their stillness and treat these dear animals, as well as yourself and other people, with kindness and respect.

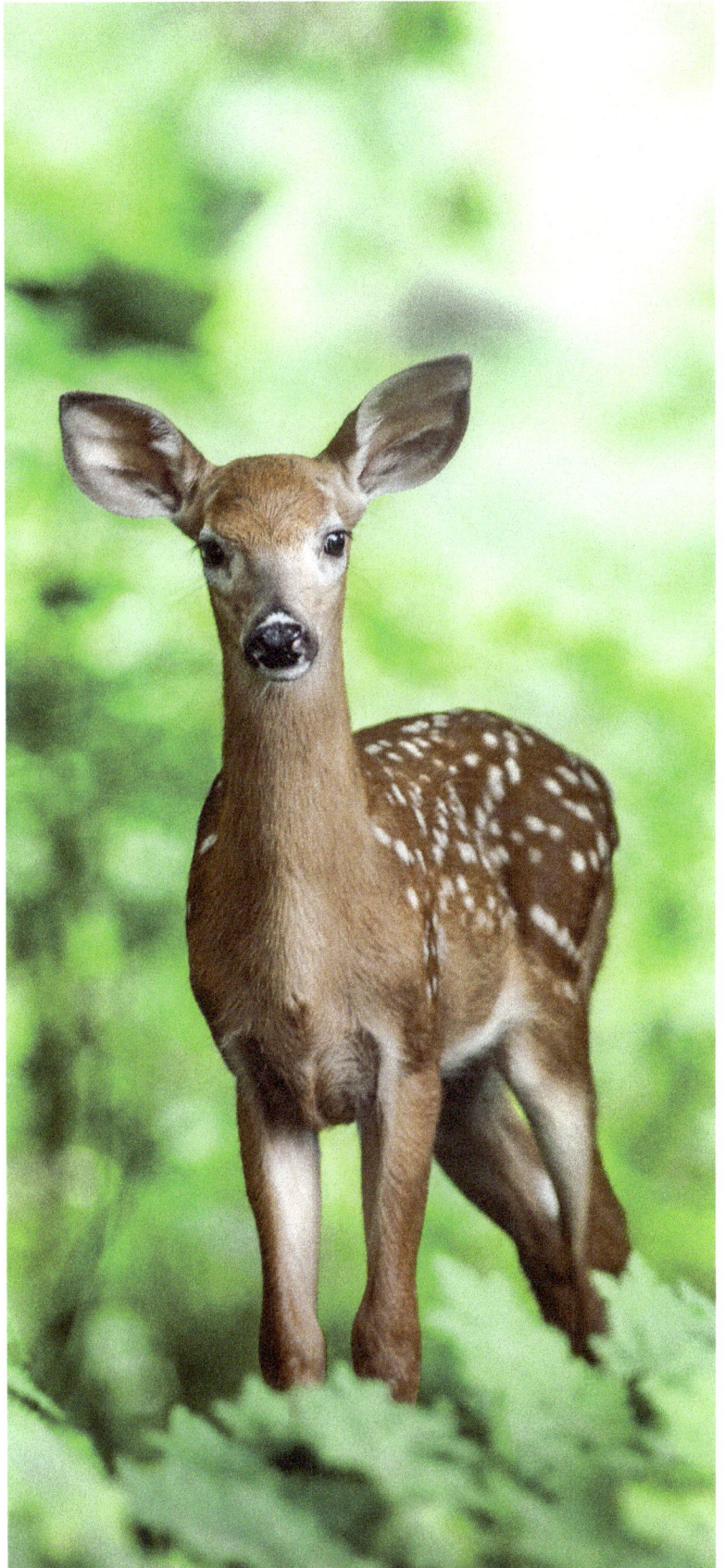

DOG

GIVE LOVE, AND YOU'LL GET LOVE

Dogs are fun and loving, great to hold and squeeze
That's why they are welcome in many families

Dogs are loving pets and loyal companions. Many dogs can also show concern and empathy—recognizing the feelings of people and staying close to their human family members in times of need. When you hold and pet dogs and treat them well, they show unconditional love, wagging their tails when happy. Show as much love as dogs do, and you will probably get a lot of love, too.

DOLPHIN

BE SENSITIVE TO THE FEELINGS OF OTHERS

Dolphins show intelligence in ways that are revealing
With judgment, solving problems, and even having feelings

Next to humans, dolphins might be the smartest mammals. They communicate, solve problems, and interact with people. (It even looks like they're smiling.) Like dogs, they show empathy—recognizing the feelings of others. They can sense when another dolphin or a person is in danger, then come to their rescue. That's a great skill to recognize and be sensitive to the feelings of others.

DOVE

ANIMALS CAN BE A REMINDER OF PEACE

Looking for a symbol of peace and love?
Look no further than the peace-loving dove

Doves are a symbol of peace and love because they are so innocent and harmless. Being pigeons, they have been used as trusted messengers, delivering letters over thousands of miles. Doves remind us of a message we must never forget—to be messengers of peace and love.

EAGLE

ANIMALS CAN TEACH US COURAGE

High up in the sky, eagles always tower
Symbols of great courage, freedom, and power

Eagles have inspired people for centuries as symbols of freedom, strength, and bravery. They are fearless, graceful, and have excellent vision. When you need the courage to raise your confidence and spread your wings, think of an eagle's ability and imagine soaring like one.

ELEPHANT

APPRECIATE YOUR MOM AND FAMILY

Elephants live in families that are large and strong
With moms who lead the way, so little can go wrong

Elephants live in groups led by mothers with strong family ties. They also have excellent memories and don't forget to care for the calves (babies) of other elephants in need. Elephants teach you to appreciate your mother's role in raising you and the importance of a loving family.

FINCH

WE ADAPT TO CHANGE TO BECOME STRONGER

We all adapt to change in order to get stronger
It's how we live a life that is healthier and longer

Small birds can inspire big discoveries. When scientist Charles Darwin studied the evolution of animal species, he looked at many types of finches on the Galapagos Islands. Each adapted to its island setting differently over time to survive. Adapt to change in order to become stronger.

GIRAFFE & SQUIRREL

LEARN TO USE THE GIFTS YOU HAVE

Giraffes are tall and squirrels short, but none has the advantage

When it comes to finding food, both know how to manage

Giraffes are the tallest mammals (19 feet), while squirrels are among the shortest (6 inches tall). Giraffes use their long necks to reach for food in trees, while squirrels are great climbers who often dash up tree trunks to get food. Learn to use the gifts you have to get what you need.

GOAT

BE CURIOUS BUT NOT CARELESS

Goats are curious creatures, always at their best
Exploring things or eating anything they can digest

Goats have never-ending curiosity. They explore everything and eat just about anything. It's great to be curious and discover new things, even if you make a little mess in the process like goats often do. But never stop exploring or asking questions. Be curious, just not careless.

HIPPO & FLAMINGO

DON'T TEASE PEOPLE WHO ARE OVERWEIGHT

Hippos are so big they can be a source of teasing
While flamingos are so beautiful, seeing them is pleasing

Hippos are huge and ungraceful, while flamingos are slender and graceful. These two animals couldn't be more different, though people still love them both. Never tease people who are overweight or love them any less. Treat everyone the same through thick and thin.

HORSE

NEVER LOSE YOUR FREE SPIRIT

Horses are by nature as wild as the wind
Even tame, they still would win most races they are in

Horses are beautiful animals, proud and tall. Their instinct is to run free and wild. Over the centuries, they've been tamed to make people's lives easier on horseback. But give them free rein, and they still love to run. No matter how tame you become, never lose your free spirit.

HUMMINGBIRD

SIZE DOESN'T MATTER

Hummingbirds are acrobats, the smallest birds in flight
Finding nectar all day for their endless appetite

Hummingbirds are the smallest migrating birds. No creature uses more energy. They eat while they are flying, finding nectar from flowers—flapping their wings up to 80 times every second. Watch a hummingbird in flight! They teach you not to worry about your size if you are small.

KANGAROO

APPRECIATE THE CLOSENESS BETWEEN A MOTHER AND CHILD

When it comes to close contact and knowing what to do
There's no better example than a mother kangaroo

There's no better baby carrier in the animal kingdom than the kangaroo. After birth, a mom moves her baby from a stressful place to a calm and secure pouch for six months, nursing and nurturing it. In humans, close contact between a mother and child is healthy and so important!

KOALA

SLEEP IS VERY IMPORTANT

There's nothing quite as restful as a koala that's asleep
So if you see one snoozing, please don't make a peep

All animals need sleep after a busy, tiring day of searching for food or, in some cases, keeping enemies away. But koalas sleep, take naps, and sleep some more—up to 20 hours each day in a tree! Maybe that's overdoing it, but we're trying to make a point. Sleep helps you stay healthy.

LION

LEARN FROM YOUR MISTAKES

We think of lions as hunters with all the skills it takes
But young lions often fail, then learn from their mistakes

Lions have total focus when hunting. But when lions first learn to hunt, they fail more than half the time. But they keep learning and prepare for the next time. If you learn from your mistakes, don't get upset. When something goes wrong, learn from it and you'll get better the next time!

MONKEY

PLAY AND BE SILLY

Monkeys love to play, and they have so much fun
There's no sillier animal, not a single one!

Monkeys love to play and be silly. They make you laugh and appreciate the pure joy of having fun. Take time to play and be silly. (But it's not polite to stick your tongue out!) You'll have plenty of time to be serious when you grow up. For now, get all the laughs you can out of life.

OCTOPUS

YOU CAN CONNECT WITH ANYONE

Some think octopuses are a strange and frightening creature
Guess they need a friendly "Octopus Teacher"

An octopus has eight arms, each with a mini-brain (a mind of its own) and a main brain. All that brainpower helps them solve problems and feel physical and emotional pain. Octopuses teach you to connect with creatures both odd and shy—and to befriend people who are different.

OTTER

STAY CLOSE TO YOUR LOVED ONES

Otters hold each other's hands as close as they can be
It helps to keep them safe instead of drifting out to sea

Otters are furry creatures who float on their backs. And how's this for "otterly" adorable? They hold hands to keep from drifting apart at sea to survive in the wild. If you hold hands with your mom, dad, or other loved ones, you'll be more likely to stay closer together—and be safer, too.

OWL

BE OBSERVANT

Owls can turn their heads almost all the way around
With eyes so keen and ears that hear nearly every sound

Owls have amazing vision, sharp hearing, and an intense stare. They are patient hunters who can turn their heads almost all the way around in a circle! They don't miss a thing! You will be better prepared for the unexpected if you always look around and are as watchful as an owl.

PANDA

LIFE IS PRECIOUS

*Don't take it for granted
when animals are alive*

*Let's protect their homes
to make sure they survive*

Pandas are one of the
most adorable animals
of all. However, pandas
and many other animals
are endangered and
teach us an important
lesson: By protecting
where they live, we can
help them live safely
and produce future
generations. Life is
precious; never take it
for granted.

PARROT

BE CAREFUL OF WHAT YOU SAY

Parrots make a lot of noise,
much of it is squawking
But when they socialize with people,
lots of them start talking

Parrots are very social birds. When they are with people, they try to imitate sounds to fit in. Many can even learn words and phrases. Be careful of what you say. Words you don't mean to say out loud can be repeated by others. (Hint: Imagine there's an invisible parrot nearby.)

PEACOCK

DRESS TO IMPRESS

When peacocks show their feathers,
everyone's impressed
It's a good idea for you to look your best

Peacocks, especially males, have attractive plumage (feathers). What a sight! Though they are one of the largest flying birds, they don't fly well at all. (When you look this good on the ground, who needs to fly?) Take time to dress nicely every once in a while—and look your very best!

PELICAN

WE ARE CONNECTED TO CREATURES FAR BACK IN TIME

Pelicans are probably the oldest birds we know
Related to the dinosaurs millions of years ago

Do you think dinosaurs are extinct? Some birds in their family are still flying high—30 million years later. Fossils show that pelicans haven't changed much since prehistoric times. Admire their beauty in flight and appreciate how we are connected to creatures far, far back in time.

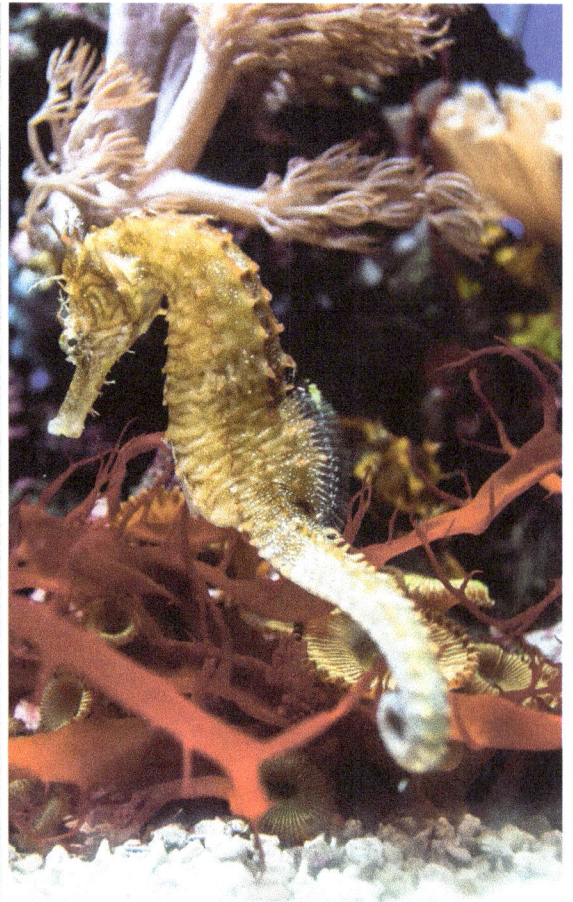

PENGUIN & SEAHORSE

BOTH PARENTS CAN SHARE IN RAISING YOU

Penguins and seahorses show that males can do their share
When it comes to helping moms with needed child care

Both penguin parents care for their offspring equally. Dad typically keeps the egg warm for weeks, in the bitter cold, until it hatches, while mom gets food. Once the chick hatches, they continue to share duties. Penguins show us both parents can have an equal role in raising you. But wait! Male seahorses actually get pregnant and give birth to their young. How cool is that!

PLATYPUS

EVERYONE IS UNIQUE AND SPECIAL

Platypuses are as strange as anything you'll see
Living proof that animals have such diversity

The puzzling platypus is a mammal, like humans, but it lays eggs, which very few mammals do. It has a duck's bill, the eyes of a fish, and it glows in the dark! Wow! Appreciate the wonders of the animal kingdom and how uniquely different all animals are. The same goes for people.

POLAR BEAR

CLIMATE CHANGE IS REAL

Saving our dear planet deserves our thought and care
And there's no greater danger sign than the threatened polar bear

Polar bears are dangerous. But they're also in danger due to global warming, which is heating the Arctic much faster than anywhere else. It melts the ice they need as a surface for hunting. Polar bears are a reminder: What can you and your family do to help reduce global warming?

RED COLOBUS

BE FRIENDLY TO YOUR NEIGHBORS

There's one type of monkey that's friendly with its neighbors
This can lead to both of them doing each other favors

The red colobus is a rare type of monkey. It is very social. It is so friendly that many socialize with other neighboring monkeys, grooming them as a way of being kind and respectful. Be friendly to your neighbors. We all need to get along with each other.

RHINO & OXPECKER

FRIENDS COME IN ALL SHAPES AND SIZES

How can birds and rhinos be friends with one another?
Because the two of them have learned to help each other

Despite their extreme size differences, rhinos have a special
relationship with a bird called the oxpecker. Rhinos attract
ticks, which suck their blood to survive. The oxpecker eats these
annoying ticks. Friends help each other, and friendships come
in all shapes, sizes, and colors.

SALMON

TRY EXTRA HARD TO REACH YOUR GOALS

Salmon have a truly awesome instinct to survive
Swimming upstream to spawn so future salmon thrive

To reproduce (*or spawn*), salmon swim upstream for miles, against strong currents, back to the streams and rivers where they were born. There they fertilize eggs laid by females, so a new generation of salmon can survive. If you want something badly enough, don't let things get in your way.

SHARK

NEVER STOP MOVING FORWARD

Sharks just keep on moving, or some will even die
If it appears they're always hunting, now you know why

Some sharks must constantly swim forward to survive, taking in oxygen from water to breathe. If they stop, their breathing shuts down, and they can die. The lesson: Never stop moving forward in life and discovering new things. (And don't forget to take breaths along the way.)

SHEEP

EVERYONE DESERVES RESPECT

Sheep eat grass and grains in pastures or in feeders
They're just fine being followers; not everyone's a leader

Sheep are followers; they rarely act on their own. That's okay.
They teach you to respect people the way they are, whether
they're leaders or followers. Everyone deserves respect,
including you. There's only one you, and you are special just
the way you are, no matter who you are.

SKUNK

FIND THE GOOD IN EVERYONE

Skunks might cause a stink with their unpleasant spray
But they help farmers keep the mice and other pests away

Skunks are known for the strong-smelling spray they use to frighten off enemies. That smelly odor has gotten them a stinky reputation. But skunks also eat mice and insects to help farmers protect their crops. Even if someone has a bad reputation, try to find the good in them.

SLOTH

DON'T POOP WHERE YOU EAT

Sloths live up in trees, hoping nobody will spoil it

The only time that they come down is to go to the toilet

Sloths live, eat, sleep, and mate in trees. Monkeys and other animals who live out on a limb poop from their branches (look out!), but not sloths. They climb down, dig a hole, and poop in it. A good bathroom habit for you: Don't poop where you eat. (And always wash your hands.)

TIGER

SOME ANIMALS EARN THEIR STRIPES

Tigers may be known for their eye-catching beauty
But these big cats have a more essential duty

Tigers live in highly threatened environments where many types of animals thrive. Because they prey on other creatures, they help control the animal population and prevent overgrazing. We need to make sure these endangered animals are protected to help maintain the balance of their environment.

TORTOISE

BEING STEADY BEATS RUSHING

Tortoises, unlike rabbits, have a slow and steady pace
But that determination can help them "win the race"

Do you know the story of "The Tortoise and the Hare?" In the end, the slow and steady tortoise wins the race over the faster but carefree hare. The moral of the story is that you are more likely to succeed if, rather than rushing, you move forward in a steady way and never give up.

WHALE

COMMUNICATION IS ESSENTIAL

Whales have different sounds they make and songs that they create
To find their way, protect their young, or help them find a mate

Communication is
vital to an animal's survival.
Whales communicate
through clicking sounds to
connect with other whales,
spot danger, teach their offspring
how to survive, or find their way.
These sounds bounce off objects,
measuring their distance, shape,
and location. Humpback whales also sing
songs to find a mate, often far, far away.
How do you communicate?

WOLF

ALWAYS LET PEOPLE KNOW WHAT YOU NEED

Wolves are skillful hunters who like to hunt in teams
To tell more wolves it's time to hunt, they go to great extremes

What's all the howling about? Wolves have an alarming howl to call other wolves to hunt with them in packs. They are excellent hunters, and together they are even better. When you let others know what you want and ask for their help, you are more likely to get what you need.

WOODPECKER

ALWAYS PROTECT YOUR HEAD

They ram their heads in tree trunks,
you'd think it causes pain

But even with the pounding,
it doesn't hurt their brain

Woodpeckers ram their heads
into trees to get insects, seeds, or
store food. How do they avoid brain
damage? Their tiny brains and tight
skulls function as a solid hammer,
leaving little room for rattling around.
You're not built that way, so wear a
helmet when cycling or skateboarding.

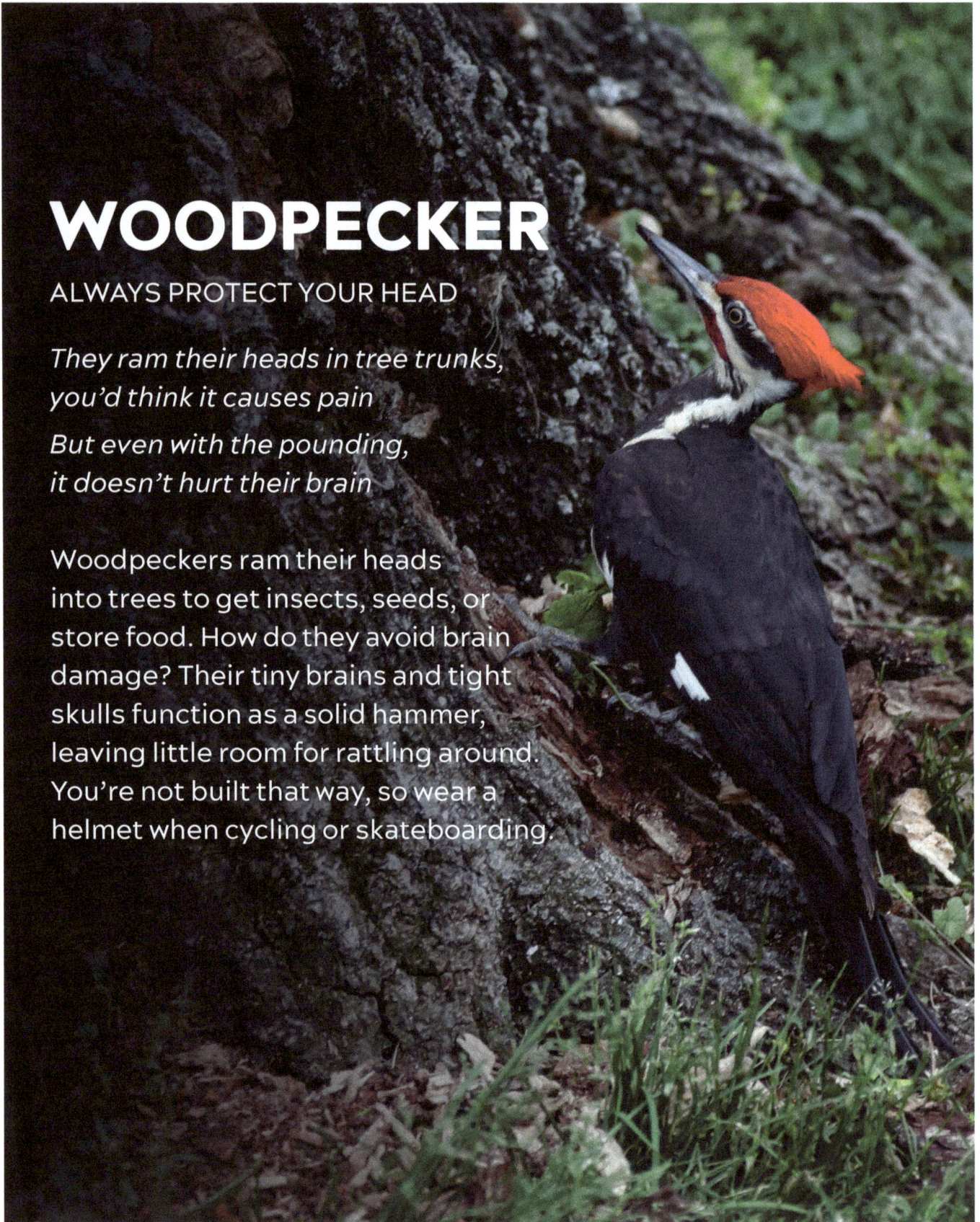

YAK

DRESS WARMLY TO PROTECT YOUR BODY

Yaks live in the mountains where it's often freezing
Covered by a coat so thick, you'll never see them sneezing

Yaks live in the highest mountains of any mammal. They have a warm, thick undercoat covered by long, bushy outer hair. This helps them survive extreme temperatures of up to 40 degrees below zero. Brrr! Yaks remind you to dress warmly to protect your body from the cold.

ZEBRA

BLACK AND WHITE TOGETHER CREATE HARMONY

Zebras are so beautiful it is plain to see
Black and white together create such harmony

A zebra is in the wild horse family. Its black and white stripes together make the zebra stand out as one of the most beautiful animals in the wild. They also remind us that black and white together can create harmony, not only in the animal kingdom, but also among different people.

Animal **"BUTTS with a Smile"** by Danny Koffman

THE STORY BEHIND THE BOOK

50 Things Animals Can Teach Us grew out of the love my wife, Jackie, and I have for animals, especially our late 20-year-old Abyssinian cat named Bisou (French for "kiss"). We shared many precious moments and kisses and learned so much from him.

Today, animals are still a big part of our lives. In our backyard, hummingbirds hover between plants and feeders, butterflies dine on milkweed, and squirrels think they own the place. On the adjoining hills, owls, deer, coyotes, and an occasional bobcat visit, while hawks, herons, and egrets fly overhead. We never forget that we are living in their space just as they are living in ours.

ABOUT THE AUTHOR

Ron Ovadia is an Irvine, California-based children's book author, lyricist, and songwriter. His current books include *A Special Kind of Family,* about the spirit of 'ohana (family) in the outrigger paddling community, and *Pelican, Pelican't*, about overcoming fear and trauma. His previous children's books include *Hank: Or How We Tried to Get Rid Of Our Ants*, a story of an overly zealous anteater, and *First Dog of 1600 Pooch'Ivania Avenue*, a dog's-eye view of the White House as told by the Obama's Portuguese Water Dog, Bo. Ron has also written many songs, including the 2022 tribute to the Ukrainian people, "Your Beloved Home," which can be found at www.ronovadiamusic.com.

CREDITS

Project management and publishing by Michael Roney, Highpoint Life. Photography sourcing: Grant Maloy Smith, Jackie Ovadia, and Sarah Clarehart. Additional original photographs: Ron Becijos and Sarah Clarehart. Editor: Chris Villaflor. A special thanks to all those who provided invaluable feedback: Kay Parker, Howard Seller, Kate Danaher Parks, Les Miller, and lastly, Rabbi Arnold Rachlis, for the impetus to complete this book.